WHAT'S COOKING?

BARBECUE

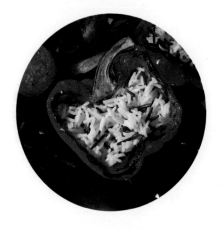

PARRAGON

First published in Great Britain in 1997 by
Parragon
Unit 13–17
Avonbridge Trading Estate
Atlantic Road
Avonmouth
Bristol BS11 9QD

ISBN: 0-7525-2258-2

Produced by Haldane Mason, London

Acknowledgements
Art Director: Ron Samuels
Editors: Jo-Anne Cox, Charles Dixon-Spain
Design: Zoë Mellors
Photography: Iain Bagwell

Printed in Italy

Material in this book has previously appeared in
Barbecues by Cara Hobday and *Vegetarian Barbecues*
by Sue Ashworth.

Note
Cup measurements in this book are for
American cups. Tablespoons are assumed to be
15 ml. Unless otherwise stated, milk is assumed
to be full fat, eggs are standard size 3 and
pepper is freshly ground black pepper.

CONTENTS

Introduction

Barbecuing is one of the simplest and most enjoyable ways of preparing food and entertaining family or friends – there is nothing like the aroma and flavour of barbecued food, and everyone can take turns at the grill. Too often, barbecues consist of only burgers and sausages, but it takes very little effort to provide a delicious range of meat, fish and vegetable dishes to suit every palate.

In this book you will find a carefully selected array of dishes which are arranged in the order they would be eaten at a barbecue. Each recipe is especially designed to take full advantage of the succulent flavour that cooking over a barbecue gives, whether that barbecue is of the disposable kind or a deluxe brick-built version.

When cooking on a barbecue, a number of factors should be considered. The first is safety: if children are going to be present at the barbecue, it is advisable that either the cooking area is out of reach for the small ones, or that an adult is always on hand, even when the cooking is finished. The fuels and types of barbecues available do vary quite considerably, so when choosing consider the numbers you will be cooking for, the regularity of your barbecues, and the space you have available outside. One major problem with barbecues is actually lighting them: try kindling, knotted paper, starter fluid or solid paraffin brickettes, but remember, fires need a flow of oxygen, so make sure your barbecue is well ventilated. Tools that you may find useful when cooking over a barbecue are metal tongs for turning food, heavy-duty gloves, a plastic wipe-clean apron, a basting brush, a water pistol or plant spray to dowse flames, a long fork, and skewers.

With variety and taste being the major criteria in choosing the recipes in this book, there are delicious and tempting dishes even for vegetarians, like Stuffed Red (Bell) Peppers and Filled Jacket Potatoes. All the recipes can be adapted to suit your needs, your barbecue and your guests.

Heavenly Garlic Dip with Crudités

Anyone who loves garlic will adore this dip. Keep it warm to one side of the barbecue, and dip raw vegetables or hunks of French bread into it.

SERVES 4

2 bulbs garlic, chopped finely • 6 tbsp olive oil
1 small onion, chopped finely
2 tbsp lemon juice
3 tbsp tahini (sesame seed paste)
2 tbsp chopped fresh parsley
salt and pepper

To serve:
fresh vegetable crudités
French bread or warmed pitta (pocket) breads

1 Separate the bulbs of garlic into cloves. Place them on a baking (cookie) sheet and roast in a preheated oven at 200°C/400°F/Gas Mark 6 for 8–10 minutes. Leave to cool for a few minutes. Peel the garlic cloves, then chop them finely.

2 Heat the olive oil in a saucepan or frying pan (skillet) and add the garlic and onion. Fry for 8–10 minutes until softened. Remove the pan from the heat.

3 Mix the lemon juice, tahini (sesame seed paste) and parsley into the garlic mixture. Season to taste with salt and pepper. Transfer to a small heatproof bowl and keep warm at one side of the barbecue.

4 Serve with a selection of fresh vegetable crudités, chunks of French bread or warm pitta (pocket) breads.

Tzatziki with Pitta (Pocket) Breads & Black Olive Dip

Tzatziki is a Greek dish, made with natural yogurt, mint and cucumber.

SERVES 4

½ cucumber
250 g/8 oz/1 cup thick natural yogurt
1 tbsp chopped fresh mint
salt and pepper • 4 pitta (pocket) breads

Black olive dip:
2 garlic cloves, crushed
125 g/4 oz/¾ cup pitted black olives
4 tbsp olive oil • 2 tbsp lemon juice
1 tbsp chopped fresh parsley

To garnish:
sprigs of fresh mint • sprigs of fresh parsley

1 To make the tzatziki, peel the cucumber and chop roughly. Sprinkle with salt and leave to stand for 15–20 minutes. Rinse with cold water and drain well. Mix the cucumber, yogurt and mint together. Season with salt and pepper and transfer to a serving bowl. Cover and leave to chill for 20–30 minutes.

2 To make the dip, put the crushed garlic and olives into a blender or food processor and blend for 15–20 seconds. Add the olive oil, lemon juice and parsley and blend for a few seconds. Alternatively, chop the garlic and olives very finely. Mix the olive oil, lemon juice and parsley with the garlic and olives and mash together. Season with salt and pepper.

3 Wrap the pitta (pocket) breads in foil and place over the barbecue for 2–3

minutes, turning once to warm through. Alternatively, heat in the oven or under the grill (broiler). Cut the bread into pieces and serve with the tzatziki and black olive dip, garnished with sprigs of fresh mint and parsley.

Filled Jacket Potatoes

Wrap the cooked potatoes in foil and keep them warm at the edge of the barbecue, ready to serve with a choice of fillings.

EACH DRESSING SERVES 4

4 large or 8 medium baking potatoes

Mexican sweetcorn relish:
250 g/8 oz can of sweetcorn, drained
½ red (bell) pepper, cored, deseeded and chopped finely
5 cm/2 inch piece of cucumber, chopped finely
½ tsp chilli powder • salt and pepper

Blue cheese, celery & chive filling:
125 g/4 oz/½ cup full-fat soft cheese
125 g/4 oz/½ cup natural fromage frais
125 g/4 oz Danish blue cheese, cut into cubes
1 celery stick, chopped finely
2 tsp snipped fresh chives • celery • salt and pepper

Mushrooms in spicy tomato sauce:
30 g/1 oz/2 tbsp butter or margarine
250 g/8 oz button mushrooms
150 g/5 oz/⅔ cup natural yogurt
1 tbsp tomato purée (paste)
2 tsp mild curry powder • salt and pepper
paprika or chilli powder, or chopped fresh herbs, to garnish

1 Scrub the potatoes and prick them with a fork. Bake in a preheated oven at 200°C/400°F/Gas Mark 6 for about 1 hour, until just tender. Wrap the potatoes in foil and keep warm.

2 To make the Mexican sweetcorn relish, put half the sweetcorn into a bowl. Put the remainder into a blender or food processor and blend for 10–15 seconds or chop and mash roughly by

hand. Add the puréed sweetcorn, (bell) pepper, cucumber and chilli powder to the sweetcorn kernels in the bowl. Season to taste.

3 To make the blue cheese, celery & chive filling, mix the soft cheese and fromage frais together until smooth. Add the blue cheese, celery and chives, and mix. Season with pepper and celery salt.

4 To make the mushrooms in spicy tomato sauce, melt the butter or margarine in a frying pan (skillet). Add the mushrooms and cook gently for 3–4 minutes. Remove from the heat and stir in the yogurt, tomato purée (paste) and curry powder. Season to taste.

5 Serve the potatoes with your choice of fillings and garnish with paprika or herbs.

Melted Cheese & Onion Baguettes

**Part-baked baguettes are filled with a
cheese and onion mixture, then cooked
over the barbecue to make them crisp.**

SERVES 4

*4 part-baked baguettes • 2 tbsp tomato relish
60 g/ 2 oz/ 4 tbsp butter
8 spring onions (scallions), trimmed and chopped finely
125 g/ 4 oz/ ½ cup cream cheese
125 g/ 4 oz/ 1¾ cups Cheddar cheese, grated
1 tsp snipped fresh chives • pepper*

To serve:
mixed salad leaves (greens) • fresh herbs

1 Split the baguettes in half
lengthways, without
cutting right through. Spread
a little tomato relish on each
split baguette.

2 Melt the butter in a frying
pan (skillet) and add the
spring onions (scallions). Fry
gently until softened and
golden. Remove from the heat
and leave to cool slightly.

3 Beat the cream cheese in
a mixing bowl to soften it.
Mix in the spring onions
(scallions), with any remaining
butter. Add the grated cheese

and snipped chives, mix well
and season.

4 Divide the cheese mixture
between the baguettes,
spread it over the cut surfaces
and sandwich together. Wrap
each baguette tightly in foil.

5 Heat the baguettes over
the barbecue for about
10–15 minutes, turning them
occasionally. Peel back the foil
to check that they are cooked
and the cheese mixture has
melted. Serve with salad
leaves (greens) and garnished
with fresh herbs.

Salmon Fillet on a Bed of Herbs

This is a great party dish, as the salmon is cooked in one piece. Even though it is cooked on a layer of herbs, it manages to keep a smoky, barbecued flavour.

SERVES 4

½ large bunch dried thyme
5 fresh rosemary branches, 15–20 cm/6–8 inches long
8 bay leaves
1 kg/2 lb salmon fillet
1 bulb fennel, cut into 8 pieces
2 tbsp lemon juice
2 tbsp olive oil

1 Make a base on a hot barbecue with the dried thyme, rosemary branches and bay leaves, overlapping them so that they cover a slightly bigger area than the salmon fillet.

2 Place the salmon on top of the herbs.

3 Arrange the pieces of fennel around the edge of the salmon.

4 Combine the lemon juice and oil and brush over the salmon with it.

5 Cover the salmon loosely with a piece of foil, to keep it moist.

6 Cook the salmon for about 20–30 minutes, basting frequently with the lemon juice mixture.

7 Remove the salmon from the barbecue, cut it into slices and serve with the fennel pieces.

Scallop Skewers

Frozen scallops are fine to use for this recipe. Serve with a rocket (arugula) salad to emphasize the Californian origin of the dish.

SERVES 4

8 wooden skewers • grated zest and juice of 2 limes
2 tbsp finely chopped lemon grass or 1 tbsp lemon juice
2 garlic cloves, crushed
1 green chilli, deseeded and chopped
16 scallops, with corals • 2 limes, each cut into 8 segments
2 tbsp sunflower oil • 1 tbsp lemon juice
salt and pepper

To serve:
60 g / 2 oz / 1 cup rocket (arugula) salad
200 g / 7 oz / 3 cups mixed salad leaves (greens)

1 Soak the skewers in warm water for at least 20 minutes before you use them.

2 Meanwhile, combine the lime zest and juice, lemon grass or lemon juice, garlic and chilli together in a pestle and mortar or spice grinder to make a paste.

3 Whisk together the oil, lemon juice, salt and pepper thoroughly to make the salad dressing.

4 Thread 2 scallops on to each of the soaked skewers, alternating with 2 lime segments.

5 Coat the scallops with the spice paste and place over a medium-hot barbecue, basting occasionally. Cook for 10 minutes, turning once.

6 Toss the rocket (arugula), mixed salad leaves (greens) and dressing together.

7 Serve the scallops piping hot, 2 skewers on each plate, with the rocket (arugula) and salad leaves (greens).

Sea Bass Baked in Foil

Sea bass is often paired with subtle oriental flavours. For a special occasion, you may like to bone the fish, so that your guests can cut straight through the flesh.

SERVES 4–6

2 sea bass, about 1 kg/2 lb each, gutted and scaled
2 spring onions (scallions), green part only, cut into strips
5 cm/2 inch piece of ginger, peeled and cut into strips
2 garlic cloves, unpeeled, crushed lightly
2 tbsp mirin or dry sherry
salt and pepper

To serve:
pickled sushi ginger (optional)
soy sauce

1 For each fish lay out a double thickness of foil. Oil the top piece of foil well, or lay a piece of silicon paper over the foil. Place the fish in the middle and expose the cavity.

2 Divide the spring onions (scallions) and ginger between each cavity. Put a garlic clove in each cavity. Pour over the mirin or dry sherry. Season the fish well.

3 Close the cavities and lay each fish on its side. Fold over the foil and seal the edges together securely. Fold each end neatly.

4 Cook the fish over a medium-hot barbecue for 15 minutes, turning once.

5 To serve, remove the foil and cut each fish into 2 or 3 pieces. Serve with the pickled ginger, if using, accompanied by soy sauce.

Swordfish Steak with Roast Garlic

On a Saturday morning the fish market in Sydney is packed with people buying fish for their weekend 'barbies', and swordfish is a very popular choice.

SERVES 4

4 swordfish steaks, about 200 g / 7 oz each
4 tbsp olive oil
2 whole garlic bulbs
pepper

1 Brush the swordfish steaks with the olive oil and season well. Set aside.

2 Cook the whole unpeeled garlic bulbs over a very hot barbecue for about 25 minutes until they are soft to the touch. It is difficult to overcook the garlic, but keep an eye on it nevertheless.

3 After the garlic has been cooking for about 15 minutes, put the steaks on the barbecue and cook for 5–6 minutes on each side, until the flesh is firm and flakes easily. Brush once or twice with the olive oil during cooking.

4 When the garlic is soft to the touch, cut across the top of it, exposing all the cloves.

5 When the swordfish steaks are cooked, place on a serving plate. Squeeze the garlic cloves out of their skins and rub all over liberally. Season with pepper and serve immediately.

Baby Octopus & Squid with Chilli Sauce

This is a delicious and unusual recipe, best served with a simple green salad.

SERVES 4–6

150 ml/¼ pint/⅔ cup rice vinegar
50 ml/2 fl oz/¼ cup dry sherry
2 red chillies, deseeded and chopped • 1 tsp sugar • 4 tbsp oil
12 baby octopus • 12 small squid tubes, cleaned
2 spring onions (scallions), sliced • 1 garlic clove, crushed
2.5 cm/1 inch piece ginger, grated
4 tbsp sweet chilli sauce • salt

1 Combine the vinegar, sherry, chillies, sugar, 2 tbsp of the oil and a pinch of salt in a large bowl.

2 Wash each octopus under cold running water and drain. Lay each on its side on a chopping board. Remove the head and beak and discard. Put the tentacles, which should all be in one piece, into the vinegar mixture with the squid tubes. Cover and chill for 8 hours or overnight.

3 Put the remaining oil into a frying pan (skillet) or wok and add the spring onions (scallions), garlic and ginger. Stir for 1 minute over a very hot barbecue. Remove from the heat and add the chilli sauce. Set aside.

4 Drain the fish from the marinade. Cut the pointed bottom end off each squid tube, so that you are left with tubes of even width all the way down. Make a cut down one side and open out the squid so that it is flat. Make four cuts in one direction and four in the other to create a lattice pattern.

5 Cook the octopus and squid over the hottest part of the barbecue for 4–5 minutes, turning constantly.

The octopus tentacles will curl up, and are cooked when the flesh is no longer translucent. The squid tubes will curl back on themselves, revealing the lattice cuts.

When cooked, toss them into the pan with the chilli sauce to coat and serve immediately.

Filipino Chicken

Tomato ketchup is used in this recipe from the Philippines. It is a very popular ingredient as it has a zingy sweet-sour flavour.

SERVES 4

1 can of lemonade or lime-and-lemonade
2 tbsp gin
4 tbsp tomato ketchup
2 tsp garlic salt
2 tsp Worcestershire sauce
4 chicken supremes or breasts
salt and pepper

To serve:
thread egg noodles
1 green chilli, chopped finely
2 spring onions (scallions), sliced

1 Combine the lemonade or lime-and-lemonade, gin, tomato ketchup, garlic salt, Worcestershire sauce and seasoning in a large non-porous dish.

2 Add the chicken pieces to the dish, ensuring they are covered completely.

3 Cover and put in the refrigerator to marinate for 2 hours. Allow to come to room temperature for 30 minutes before cooking.

4 Cook the chicken over a medium-hot barbecue for 20 minutes, turning once, until completely cooked through.

5 Remove the chicken from the barbecue and leave to rest for 3–4 minutes.

6 Carve into thin slices and serve with egg noodles, tossed with a little green chilli and spring onions (scallions).

Mediterranean Grilled Chicken

This recipe from the Languedoc area of France uses crisp, juicy chicken.

SERVES 4

4 tbsp natural yogurt
3 tbsp sun-dried tomato paste
1 tbsp olive oil
15 g/½ oz/¼ cup fresh basil leaves, lightly crushed
2 garlic cloves, roughly chopped
4 chicken quarters
coarse sea salt
green salad, to serve

1 Combine the yogurt, tomato paste, olive oil, basil leaves and garlic in a small bowl and mix well.

2 Put the marinade into a bowl large enough to hold the chicken quarters in a single layer. Add the chicken quarters, making sure they are thoroughly coated in the marinade.

3 Leave the chicken to marinate in the refrigerator for at least 2 hours or overnight. Remove and leave, covered, at room temperature for 30 minutes before cooking.

4 Grill (broil) the chicken over a medium-hot barbecue for 30–40 minutes, turning frequently.

5 Check the meat is cooked by piercing the flesh at the top of the drumstick. If the juices run clear, the chicken is cooked. If the juices are pink, cook for another 10 minutes.

6 Sprinkle with coarse sea salt and serve hot or cold with a green salad.

Blackened Chicken with Guacamole

This easy recipe is typical of French Cajun cooking which has its roots in earthy, strong flavours, and uses plenty of spice.

SERVES 4

4 skinless, boneless chicken breasts
60 g/2 oz/¼ cup butter, melted

Spice mix:
1 tsp salt • 1 tbsp sweet paprika
1 tsp dried onion granules
1 tsp dried garlic granules
1 tsp dried thyme • 1 tsp cayenne
½ tsp cracked black pepper • ½ tsp dried oregano

Guacamole:
1 avocado • 1 tbsp lemon juice • 2 tbsp soured cream
½ red onion, chopped • 1 garlic clove, halved

1 Put the chicken breasts between two pieces of clingfilm (plastic wrap), and pound with a mallet or rolling pin to an even thickness. They should be about 1 cm/½ inch thick. Brush each chicken breast all over with the melted butter, then set aside.

2 Combine the spice mix ingredients in a bowl. Dip the chicken breasts in the spice mix, ensuring that they are well coated. Set aside.

3 To make the guacamole, mash the avocado with the lemon juice in a small bowl. Stir in the soured cream and onion. Wipe the garlic clove around the guacamole serving dish, pressing hard. Spoon in the guacamole.

4 Place the chicken breasts over the hottest part of a

very hot barbecue and cook
for 8–10 minutes, turning
once. Slice the breasts into
thick pieces and serve
immediately, accompanied by
the guacamole.

Chargrilled Chicken Salad

This is a quick dish to serve as a starter to your hungry guests. If the bread is bent in half, the chicken salad can be put in the middle and eaten as finger food.

SERVES 4

2 skinless, boneless chicken breasts
1 red onion • oil for brushing
1 avocado, pitted • 1 tbsp lemon juice
120 ml/4 fl oz/½ cup mayonnaise
¼ tsp chilli powder
½ tsp pepper • ¼ tsp salt
4 tomatoes, quartered
1 round sun-dried tomato-flavoured focaccia bread
green salad, to serve

1 Cut the chicken breasts into 1 cm/½ inch strips.

2 Cut the onion into eight pieces, held together at the root. Rinse under cold running water, pat dry and brush with oil.

3 Purée or mash the avocado and lemon juice together. Whisk in the mayonnaise. Add the chilli powder, pepper and salt.

4 Grill (broil) the chicken and onion over a hot barbecue for 3–4 minutes on each side until just beginning to blacken.

5 Combine the blackened chicken and onion with the avocado mixture, then stir in the tomatoes.

6 Cut the focaccia into four quarters, then slice each quarter in half horizontally. Toast on the hot barbecue for about 2 minutes on each side. Spoon the chicken mixture over the toasts and serve with a green salad.

Tasmanian Duck

Some of the best cherries in the world are grown in Tasmania, hence the name of this recipe, though dried cherries from any country can be used.

SERVES 4

4 duck breasts • 60 g/ 2 oz/ ½ cup dried cherries
120 ml/ 4 fl oz/ ½ cup water • 4 tbsp lemon juice
2 large leeks, quartered, or 8 baby leeks
2 tbsp olive oil • 2 tbsp balsamic vinegar
2 tbsp port • 2 tsp pink peppercorns

1 Make 3 slashes in the fat of the duck breasts in one direction, and 3 in the other.

2 Put the dried cherries, water and lemon juice into a small saucepan. Bring to the boil. Remove from the heat and leave to cool.

3 Turn a foil tray upside-down, make several holes in the bottom and place it, right side up, over a hot barbecue.

4 Put the duck into the tray. Cover with foil and cook for 20 minutes.

5 Brush the leeks with oil and cook on the open barbecue for 5–7 minutes, turning constantly.

6 Remove the duck from the tray and cook on the open barbecue for 5 minutes, skin-side down, while you make the sauce.

7 Stir the balsamic vinegar into the cooking sauces in the tray, scraping any bits from the bottom. Add to the cherries in the saucepan. Return to the heat – either the hob (stove top) or barbecue – and stir in the port and pink peppercorns. Bring to the boil and cook for 5 minutes, until the sauce has thickened slightly.

8 Serve the duck piping hot, pour over the cherries and sauce, and accompany with the leeks.

Tex-Mex Ribs

The best ribs are those from the Jacob's Ladder, between the 1st and 5th rib.

SERVES 4–6

250 ml/ 8 fl oz/ 1 cup tomato ketchup
50 ml/ 2 fl oz/ ¼ cup cider vinegar
60 g/ 2 oz/ ⅓ cup light muscovado sugar
1 onion, chopped • 3 garlic cloves, crushed
1 tbsp dried chilli flakes • 2 tbsp Dijon mustard
1 tsp Worcestershire sauce • 2 kg/ 4 lb beef ribs

To serve:
1 French baguette, sliced • 125 g/ 4 oz/ ½ cup butter
3 garlic cloves, crushed • 1 tbsp chopped fresh parsley
1 avocado • lemon juice
250 g/ 8 oz mixed salad leaves (greens) • salt and pepper

1 Combine the ketchup, vinegar, sugar, onion, garlic, chilli flakes, mustard and Worcestershire sauce in a saucepan. Bring to the boil, and simmer for 10 minutes.

2 Wrap the ribs in foil, either in one piece or 3–4 smaller parcels. Cook over a medium-hot barbecue for 10 minutes, turning once or twice.

3 Meanwhile, combine the butter, garlic and parsley with plenty of salt and pepper. Spread the butter between each slice of the baguette and wrap in foil.

4 Peel and dice the avocado. Sprinkle over the lemon juice and mix together with the salad leaves.

5 Unwrap the ribs and place over the hot barbecue. Baste with the ketchup mixture. Cook for 20 minutes, turning occasionally. Meanwhile, cook the garlic bread for 15–20 minutes. Serve the ribs hot, with any leftover sauce for dipping, the garlic bread and the salad.

Provençale Grilled Beef

This recipe makes use of a coarse-grained but very tasty cut of beef called a hanging skirt, rump skirt or butcher's cut. You will find that it is very reasonably priced.

SERVES 6–8

1 kg/ 2 lb rump skirt or rump steak
½ tsp pepper
4 tbsp French olive oil
6 anchovies, chopped finely
2 garlic cloves, chopped finely
2 tbsp chopped fresh flat-leafed (Italian) parsley
2 tsp sea salt
French bread, to serve

1 With a sharp knife, trim any excess fat from the meat. Pare off any membrane or connective tissue, which will misshape the meat as it cooks.

2 Rub pepper and 1 tbsp of the olive oil all over the meat. Cover and chill for about 2 hours.

3 Combine the anchovies, garlic, parsley, sea salt and the remaining olive oil.

4 Remove the meat from the refrigerator 30 minutes before cooking.

5 Place the meat over a hot barbecue. Cook for 8 minutes, then turn over and spread the anchovy mix on the top side. Cook the other side for 6 minutes.

6 When the meat is cooked, transfer to a chopping board. Leave to rest for 1 minute before slicing thinly.

7 Transfer to a warmed serving platter and serve with the French bread.

Steak in Red Wine Marinade

The steak should be between 2.5 cm/1 inch and 7 cm/3 inches thick. Fillet, sirloin and entrecôte are also suitable, although rump retains the most flavour.

SERVES 4

4 rump steaks, weighing about 250 g/8 oz each
600 ml/1 pint/2½ cups red wine
1 onion, quartered • 2 tbsp Dijon mustard
2 garlic cloves, crushed
4 large field mushrooms
olive oil for brushing • salt and pepper
branch of fresh rosemary (optional)

1 Snip through the fat strip on the steaks in 3 places, so that the steak retains its shape when barbecued.

2 Combine the red wine, onion, mustard, garlic, and salt and pepper. Lay the steaks in a shallow non-porous dish and pour over the marinade. Cover and chill for 2–3 hours.

3 Remove the steaks from the refrigerator 30 minutes before you intend to cook them to let them come to room temperature. This is especially important if the steak is thick, to ensure that it cooks more evenly and is not well done on the outside and raw in the middle.

4 Sear both sides of the steak – about 1 minute on each side – over a hot barbecue. If it is about 2.5 cm/1 inch thick, keep it over a hot barbecue, and cook for about 4 minutes on each side. This will give a medium-rare steak – cook it more or less, to suit your taste. (If the steak is a thicker cut that needs thorough cooking, move it to a less hot part of the barbecue or further away

from the coals and complete cooking.) To test the readiness of the meat while cooking, simply press it with your finger – the more the meat yields, the less it is cooked.

5 Brush the mushrooms with the olive oil and cook them alongside the steak, for 5 minutes, turning once. When you put the mushrooms on the barbecue, put the rosemary branch, if using, on the fire to flavour the meat slightly. Remove the steak and leave to rest for 1–2 minutes before serving. Slice the mushrooms and serve alongside the steak.

Beef Patties

The traditional beefburger needs no egg to hold it together. Do not be tempted to use extra-lean meat as the result will be too dry; any excess fat will drain off anyway.

SERVES 4

500 g/ 1 lb minced (ground) beef
250 g/ 8 oz/ 1 cup minced (ground) lamb
1 onion, chopped finely • 4 soft hamburger buns
½ iceberg lettuce, shredded • 4 gherkins
mustard • salt and pepper

Salsa:

6 tomatoes, halved • 1 red onion, chopped finely
1 red chilli, deseeded and chopped
2 tbsp dark brown sugar
50 ml/ 2 fl oz/¼ cup cider vinegar
1 tsp balsamic or sherry vinegar • salt and pepper
2 tbsp chopped fresh chervil (optional)

1 Combine the beef, lamb and onion in a large bowl and season. Divide the mixture into 4 and make 1 ball from each quarter. To ensure that the patties have no air pockets, throw each ball between your cupped hands several times to compact the mixture, until you have a dense ball of meat. Put each ball on a plate and press down gently with the palm of your hand to make it into a patty. Chill.

2 To make the salsa, bake the tomato halves in a preheated oven at 180°C/ 350°F/Gas Mark 4 for 40–50 minutes until collapsed. Chop the tomato coarsely and combine with the onion, chilli, sugar, vinegars and chervil. Season and transfer to a serving dish.

3 Cook the patties over a hot barbecue for 10 minutes, turning once. This will give a medium-rare

burger – for a well-done burger, cook for 15 minutes. Towards the end of cooking time, split the soft hamburger buns and toast lightly on the barbecue for 1–2 minutes on the cut side.

4 Put some shredded lettuce, the beefburger, a gherkin and mustard to taste on the bottom half of the toasted bun, and cover with the top half. Serve with the tomato salsa.

Lamb Fillet with Roasted Baby Onions

This dish should be marinated overnight to tenderize the lamb. It also ensures that the flavours seep into the meat and keep it moist during cooking.

SERVES 6–8

500 g/1 lb lamb neck fillet
500 g/1 lb pickling (pearl) onions
1 tbsp olive oil • 3 tbsp chopped fresh thyme
2 lemons, rinsed and sliced thickly

Marinade:
4 tbsp olive oil • 3 garlic cloves, well crushed
½ tsp salt • ½ tsp pepper

1 To make the marinade, mix all of the ingredients together to form a paste. Smear the paste all over the lamb fillet and leave to marinate overnight in the refrigerator.

2 Cook the onions in a saucepan of boiling water for 15 minutes, until almost cooked through. Peel them.

3 Heat the oil and thyme in a frying pan (skillet) and add the onions to reheat them and coat them in the oil and thyme. Set aside.

4 Lay the lemon slices over a very hot barbecue. Place the lamb on top and cook for 10 minutes on each side, basting frequently.

5 Meanwhile, put the onions on the grid around the lamb and cook for 10 minutes, turning often until they are quite soft but charred on the outside. Serve the lamb with the onions.

Kleftiko

This classic Greek dish is usually made with leg of lamb. Keep an eye on the barbecue to ensure the heat remains even during cooking.

SERVES 6–8

1 kg/ 2 lb leg of lamb, boned and butterflied
5 garlic cloves, sliced
2 large rosemary sprigs, broken into 20 short lengths
6 tbsp olive oil • 4 tbsp lemon juice
2 tbsp chopped fresh mint • ½ tsp pepper
2 aubergines (eggplants), sliced lengthways

Rice pilau:

½ onion, chopped • 2 tbsp extra virgin olive oil
175 g/ 6 oz/ ¾ cup basmati rice
300 ml/ ½ pint/ 1¼ cups chicken stock • salt and pepper
1 tbsp pine kernels (nuts) • 1 tbsp chopped fresh oregano

1 Roll the lamb into a leg shape. Tuck in the shank (thin) end and fasten in place with skewers, preferably metal. Make 20 small nicks in the skin of the lamb with a knife. Insert a garlic slice and rosemary sprig into each nick.

2 Combine 4 tbsp of the olive oil with lemon juice, mint and pepper in a saucepan. Bring to a boil. Pour the simmering marinade over the lamb and rub in. Place the lamb on a piece of double foil or in a large foil tray on the grid over a medium-hot barbecue. Cook the lamb for 15 minutes, turning frequently. Then turn every 10–15 minutes for about 1 hour, until the lamb is cooked through. You may need to change the foil during this time to avoid flare-ups. The shank end will be more well cooked than the larger end.

3 Make the rice pilau. Heat the olive oil in a saucepan,

add the onion and fry over a gentle heat until softened, about 5 minutes. Add the rice and stir until translucent. Add the stock and bring to the boil. Season well and simmer over a gentle heat for 15 minutes. Stir in the pine kernels (nuts) and oregano. Keep warm.

4 Cut a lattice pattern in the aubergine (eggplant) slices. Brush with olive oil and cook on the grid of the barbecue for 10 minutes, turning once.

5 Slice the lamb and serve with the aubergine (eggplant) and rice pilau.

Sweet & Sour Pork Ribs

This recipe uses the spare rib, the traditional Chinese-style rib. However, baby back ribs and loin ribs are also suitable.

SERVES 4–6

2 garlic cloves, crushed
5 cm / 2 inch piece of ginger, grated
150 ml / ¼ pint / ⅔ cup soy sauce
2 tbsp sugar
4 tbsp sweet sherry
4 tbsp tomato purée (paste)
300 g / 10 oz / 2 cups pineapple, cubed
2 kg / 4 lb pork spare ribs
3 tbsp clear honey
5 pineapple rings, fresh or canned

1 Combine the garlic, ginger, soy sauce, sugar, sherry, tomato purée (paste) and cubed pineapple in a non-porous dish.

2 Put the spare ribs into the dish and make sure that they are coated completely with the marinade. Cover the dish and leave to marinate at room temperature for 2 hours only.

3 Cook the ribs over a medium-hot barbecue for 30–40 minutes, brushing with the honey after 20–30 minutes. Baste with the remaining marinade frequently until cooked completely.

4 Cook the pineapple rings over the barbecue for 10 minutes, turning once.

5 Serve the ribs with the pineapple rings on the side.

Sausages

Sausages are always one of the most popular things at a barbecue. Here is how to get a good result.

SERVES 4

4 barbecue pork sausages, the double-length kind,
or 8 standard size sausages
olive oil for brushing

To serve:
1 onion
1 French baguette, cut into 4
French mustard

1 Prick the sausages all over with a fork. This not only ensures that the skin does not split, but also allows the excess fat to run out. Pork and beef sausages work very well on a barbecue as they are quite firm. Brush the sausages all over with oil – this also protects the skin.

2 Cook the sausages over a hot barbecue for 10 minutes, turning frequently. If you are using standard-sized pork sausages, they will cook in less time, and chipolatas will only take 5–7 minutes.

3 Cut the onion into 8 pieces, each piece held together by a bit of onion root. Brush with oil and cook over the barbecue for 2–3 minutes.

4 Meanwhile, insert a bread knife inside each piece of baguette. Without breaking the crust, hollow out enough bread for the sausage to fit in.

5 Spread a line of mustard through the middle of the bread. Put 2 pieces of onion in each piece of baguette and push the cooked sausage through the middle. If using standard-sized sausages, put one in each end.

Devilled New Potatoes

This is a way of giving potatoes, or any other root vegetable you have to hand, the star treatment. A barbecue needs smaller side dishes like this to keep your diners happy while they wait for the main event.

SERVES 6–8

20 cocktail sticks (toothpicks)
500 g/1 lb baby new potatoes
olive oil for brushing
10 rashers (slices) streaky bacon
20 small sage leaves

1 Soak the cocktail sticks (toothpicks) in hand-hot water for 20 minutes before using. This will prevent them from scorching during cooking.

2 Bring a pan of water to the boil and add the potatoes. Boil for 10 minutes and drain. Brush the potatoes all over with olive oil.

3 Cut each bacon rasher (slice) in half along its length. Holding each piece at one end, smooth and stretch it with the back of a knife.

4 Wrap a piece of bacon around each potato enclosing a sage leaf and securing with a cocktail stick (toothpick).

5 Cook the potatoes over a hot barbecue for 6–7 minutes, turning occasionally. Serve hot or cold.

Stuffed Red (Bell) Peppers

Stuffed (bell) peppers are a well-known dish, but this is a new version adapted for the barbecue. The roasted vegetables have a tasty Mediterranean flavour.

SERVES 4

2 red (bell) peppers, halved lengthways and deseeded
2 tomatoes, halved
2 courgettes (zucchini), sliced thinly lengthways
1 red onion, cut into 8 sections, each section held together by the root
4 tbsp olive oil
2 tbsp fresh thyme leaves
60 g/2 oz/⅓ cup mixed basmati and wild rice, cooked
salt and pepper

1 Put the halved (bell) peppers, halved tomatoes, sliced courgettes (zucchini) and onion sections on to a baking (cookie) sheet.

2 Brush the vegetables with olive oil and sprinkle over the thyme leaves.

3 Cook the (bell) pepper, onion and courgette (zucchini) over a medium-hot barbecue for 6 minutes, turning once.

4 When the (bell) peppers are cooked, put a spoonful of the cooked rice into each one, and place the onion and courgette (zucchini) on top.

5 Cook the tomato halves for 2–3 minutes only. Top each stuffed (bell) pepper with a tomato half. Season with plenty of salt and pepper and serve hot.

Roast Leeks

Use a good-quality French or Italian olive oil for this deliciously simple yet sophisticated vegetable accompaniment.

SERVES 4–6

4 leeks
3 tbsp olive oil
2 tsp balsamic vinegar
sea salt and pepper

1 Halve the leeks lengthways, so that the leek is held together by the root. Rinse the leeks thoroughly to remove any dirt or grit and dry well.

2 Brush each leek liberally with the olive oil.

3 Cook the leeks over a hot barbecue for 6–7 minutes, turning once.

4 Remove the leeks from the barbecue and brush with the balsamic vinegar.

5 Sprinkle with sea salt and pepper and serve hot or warm.

Tropical Fruit Kebabs

Sear some chunks of exotic tropical fruits over the barbecue and serve with this amazing chocolate dip.

SERVES 4

4 wooden skewers

Chocolate dip:

125 g/ 4 oz/ 4 squares plain (dark) chocolate, broken into pieces
2 tbsp golden (light corn) syrup
1 tbsp cocoa powder • 1 tbsp cornflour (cornstarch)
200 ml/ 7 fl oz / generous ³/₄ cup milk

Kebabs:

1 mango • 1 paw-paw (papaya) • 2 kiwi fruit
½ small pineapple • 1 large banana
2 tbsp lemon juice • 150 ml/ ¼ pint/ ²/₃ cup white rum

1 Soak the wooden skewers in hand-hot water for 30 minutes.

2 Put all the ingredients for the chocolate dip into a saucepan. Heat, stirring constantly, until thickened and smooth. Keep warm at the edge of the barbecue.

3 Slice the mango on each side of its large, flat stone (pit). Cut the flesh into chunks, removing the peel. Halve, deseed and peel the paw-paw (papaya) and cut it into chunks. Peel the kiwi fruit and slice into chunks. Peel and cut the pineapple into chunks. Peel and slice the banana and dip the pieces in the lemon juice.

4 Thread the pieces of fruit alternately on to the wooden skewers. Place them in a shallow dish and pour over the rum. Leave to soak up the flavour of the rum until ready to barbecue, at least 30 minutes.

5 Cook the kebabs over the hot barbecue, turning

frequently, until seared, about 2 minutes.

6 Serve, accompanied by the hot chocolate dip.

Banana & Marshmallow Melts with Butterscotch Sauce

This delicious dessert will go down a treat with everyone. Bananas and marshmallows taste fantastic with the butterscotch sauce.

SERVES 4

4 wooden skewers
4 bananas
4 tbsp lemon juice
250 g/ 8 oz packet of marshmallows

Butterscotch sauce:
125 g/ 4 oz/ ½ cup butter
125 g/ 4 oz/ ⅓ cup light muscovado sugar
125 g/ 4 oz/ ⅓ cup golden (light corn) syrup
4 tbsp hot water

1 Soak the wooden skewers in hand-hot water for 30 minutes. Slice the bananas into large chunks and dip them into the lemon juice to prevent them going brown. Thread 2 marshmallows and 1 piece of banana alternately on to each skewer.

2 To make the sauce, melt the butter, sugar and syrup together in a small saucepan. Add the hot water, stirring until blended and smooth. Do not boil or the mixture will thicken to toffee. Keep the sauce warm at the edge of the barbecue, stirring from time to time.

3 Sear the kebabs over the hot barbecue for 30–40 seconds, turning constantly, so that the marshmallows just begin to brown and melt. Serve the kebabs with some of the butterscotch sauce spooned over, or use as a dipping sauce.

Index